The Essential Book of
WEDDING MUSIC

The forty best loved
organ pieces for the happy day

Kevin
Mayhew

We hope you enjoy *The Essential Book of Wedding Music.*
Further copies are available from your local
music shop or Christian bookshop.

In case of difficulty, please contact the publisher direct by writing to:

The Sales Department
KEVIN MAYHEW LTD
Rattlesden
Bury St Edmunds
Suffolk IP30 0SZ

Phone 01449 737978
Fax 01449 737834

Please ask for our complete catalogue of outstanding Church Music.

Front Cover: *A Village Wedding* (Anon. Pears print).
Reproduced by kind permission of Fine Art Photographic Library, London.

ISSUED IN THE UNITED STATES IN 1999

This edition first published in Great Britain in 1997 by Kevin Mayhew Ltd.

© Copyright 1991, 1992, 1993, 1994, 1995, 1997 Kevin Mayhew Ltd.

ISBN 1 84003 107 7
ISMN M 57004 197 8
Catalogue No: 1400160

2 3 4 5 6 7 8 9

Printed and bound in Great Britain

Contents

BRIDAL MARCH from 'Lohengrin'

Richard Wagner (1813-1883) arr. Noel Rawsthorne

7

TRUMPET VOLUNTARY

Jeremiah Clarke (1670-1707) arr. Noel Rawsthorne

Solo Trumpet

f
Sw.

, – Gt. to Ped.

Gt. *ff*

ff broader

+ Gt. to Ped.

poco rall.

11

MARCH from 'Scipio'

George Frideric Handel (1685-1759) arr. Noel Rawsthorne

13

ST ANTHONY CHORALE

Joseph Haydn (1732-1809) arr. Noel Rawsthorne

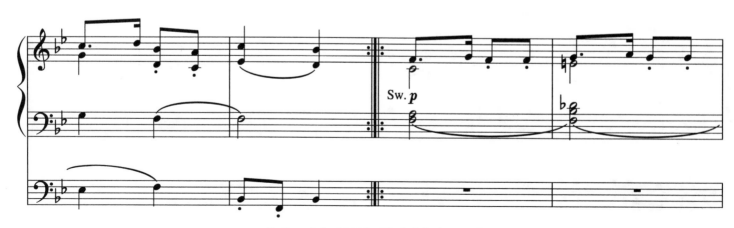

(2nd time poco rall. e dim.)

15

GAVOTTE from French Suite No. 5

Johann Sebastian Bach (1685-1750) arr. Noel Rawsthorne

ARRIVAL OF THE QUEEN OF SHEBA

George Frideric Handel (1685-1759) arr. Colin Hand

TO A WILD ROSE

Edward MacDowell (1860-1908) arr. Anthea Smith

23

For Gillian Ward Russell 16.6.94

THEME from 'JUPITER'

Gustav Holst (1874-1934) arr. Harrison Oxley

BOURRÉE from 'Water Music'

George Frideric Handel (1685-1759) arr. Noel Rawsthorne

PANIS ANGELICUS

César Franck (1822-1890) arr. Noel Rawsthorne

29

30

ARIOSO

Johann Sebastian Bach (1685-1750) arr. Colin Hand

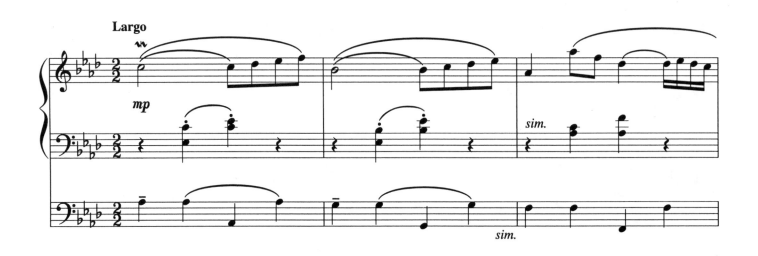

SICILIANA from Concerto No. 5

George Frideric Handel (1685-1759) arr. Noel Rawsthorne

GOD BE IN MY HEAD

Henry Walford Davies (1869-1941) arr. Noel Rawsthorne

TOCCATA in D minor BWV 565

Johann Sebastian Bach (1685-1750) edited by Alan Ridout

Prestissimo

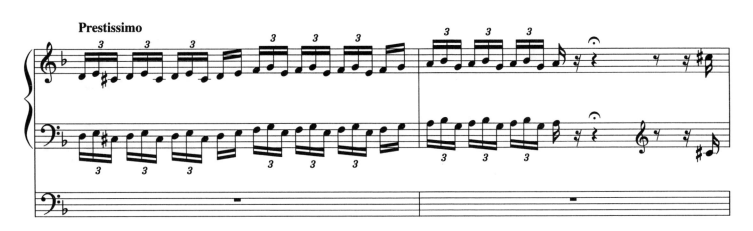

38

39

LARGO from 'Serse'

George Frideric Handel (1685-1759) arr. Noel Rawsthorne

THE SWAN

Camille Saint-Saëns (1835-1921) arr. Alexandre Guilmant (1837-1911)

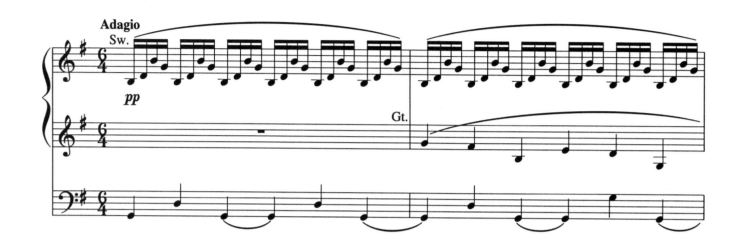

O FOR THE WINGS OF A DOVE

Felix Mendelssohn (1809-1847) arr. Alan Ridout

CANON IN D

Johann Pachelbel (1653-1706) arr. Colin Hand

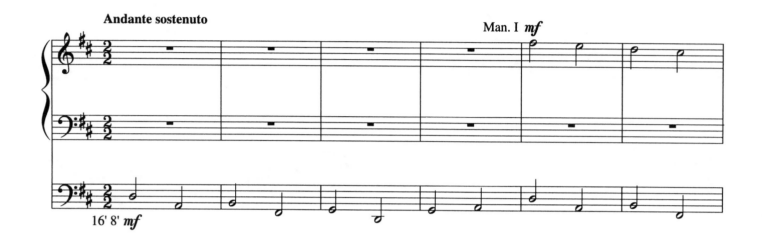

* The bass line can be played by the left hand alone if necessary.

(+Reed)

AIR from Suite No. 3

Johann Sebastian Bach (1685-1750) arr. Noel Rawsthorne

57

CHANSON DE MATIN

Edward Elgar (1857-1934) arr. Herbert Brewer (1865-1928)

CORO from 'Water Music'

George Frideric Handel (1685-1759) arr. Noel Rawsthorne

AUTUMN from 'The Four Seasons'

Antonio Vivaldi (1678-1741) arr. Alan Ridout

WEDDING MARCH from Symphony No. 3

Camille Saint-Saëns (1835-1921) arr. Martin Setchell

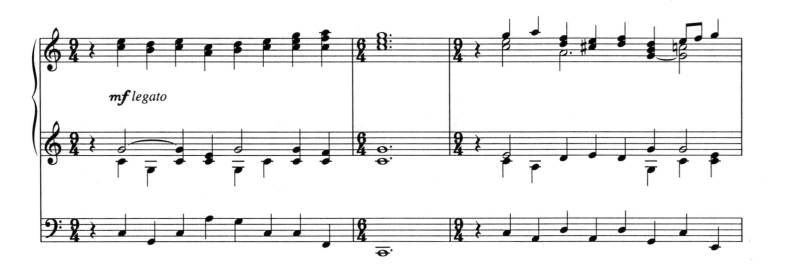

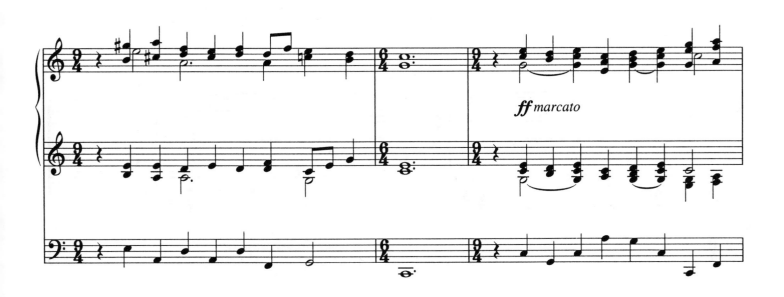

68

AVE MARIA

adapted from JS Bach by Charles Gounod (1818-1893)
arr. Anthea Smith

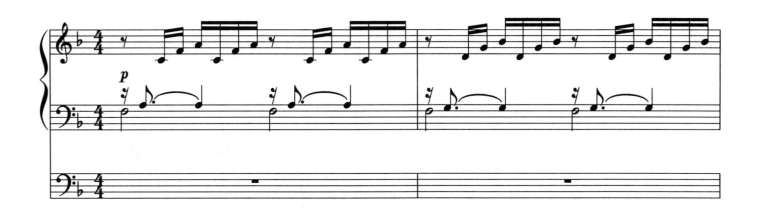

70

71

JESU, JOY OF MAN'S DESIRING

Johann Sebastian Bach (1685-1750) arr. Noel Rawsthorne

GYMNOPÉDIE I

Erik Satie (1866-1925) arr. Alan Ridout

AVE VERUM CORPUS

Wolfgang Amadeus Mozart (1756-1791) arr. Anthea Smith

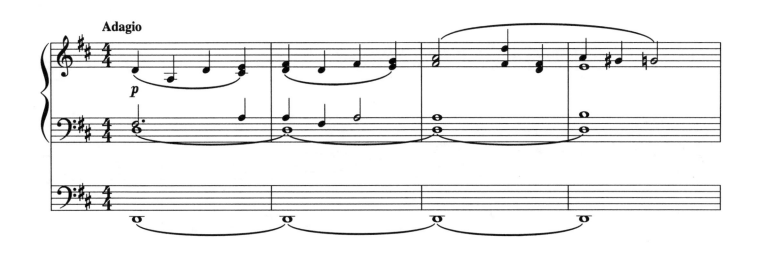

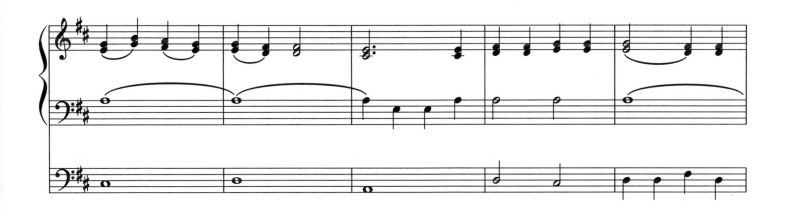

TOCCATA from Symphony 5

Charles-Marie Widor (1844-1937) arr. Colin Hand

16' 8'

(to Coda ⊕)

dim.

⊕ *For a shorter version, cut to Coda.*

poco rall.

Maestoso

ff

Reed

AIR from 'Water Music'

George Frideric Handel (1685-1759) arr. Noel Rawsthorne

SHEEP MAY SAFELY GRAZE

Johann Sebastian Bach (1685-1750) arr. Noel Rawsthorne

poco rit.

a tempo

Solo Flutes

Sw.

97

AVE MARIA

Franz Schubert (1797-1828) arr. Noel Rawsthorne

99

ODE TO JOY from Symphony No. 9

Ludwig van Beethoven (1770-1827) arr. Colin Hand

* Optional Coda, to be played *instead of* the second time bar.

FINALE from 'Music for the Royal Fireworks'

George Frideric Handel (1685-1759) arr. Noel Rawsthorne

Minuetto (♩ = 106)

8' + 2'   *mp* (repeat 8' + 4')

Man.

Gt.

107

Solo Trumpet

Accomp.

Gt.

poco rall.

109

NUN DANKET ALLE GOTT

Sigfrid Karg-Elert (1877-1933) edited by Noel Rawsthorne

GAVOTTE from Suite No. 3

Johann Sebastian Bach (1685-1750)

arr. Dom Gregory Murray (1905-1992)

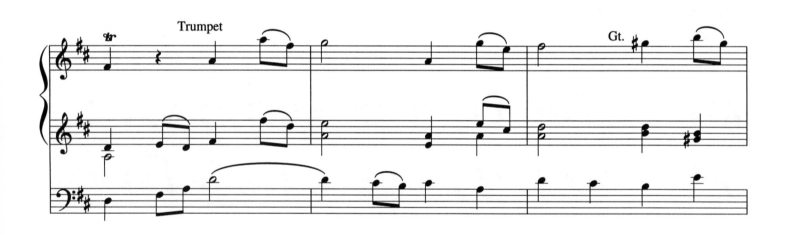

117

Fine

D.C. al Fine

NIMROD from 'Enigma Variations'

Edward Elgar (1857-1934) arr. Alan Ridout

PRELUDE from 'Te Deum'

Marc-Antoine Charpentier (1634-1704) arr. Noel Rawsthorne

125

GRAND MARCH from 'AIDA'

Giuseppe Verdi (1813-1901) arr. Colin Hand

128

129

WEDDING MARCH
from 'A Midsummer Night's Dream'

Felix Mendelssohn (1809-1847) arr. Noel Rawsthorne

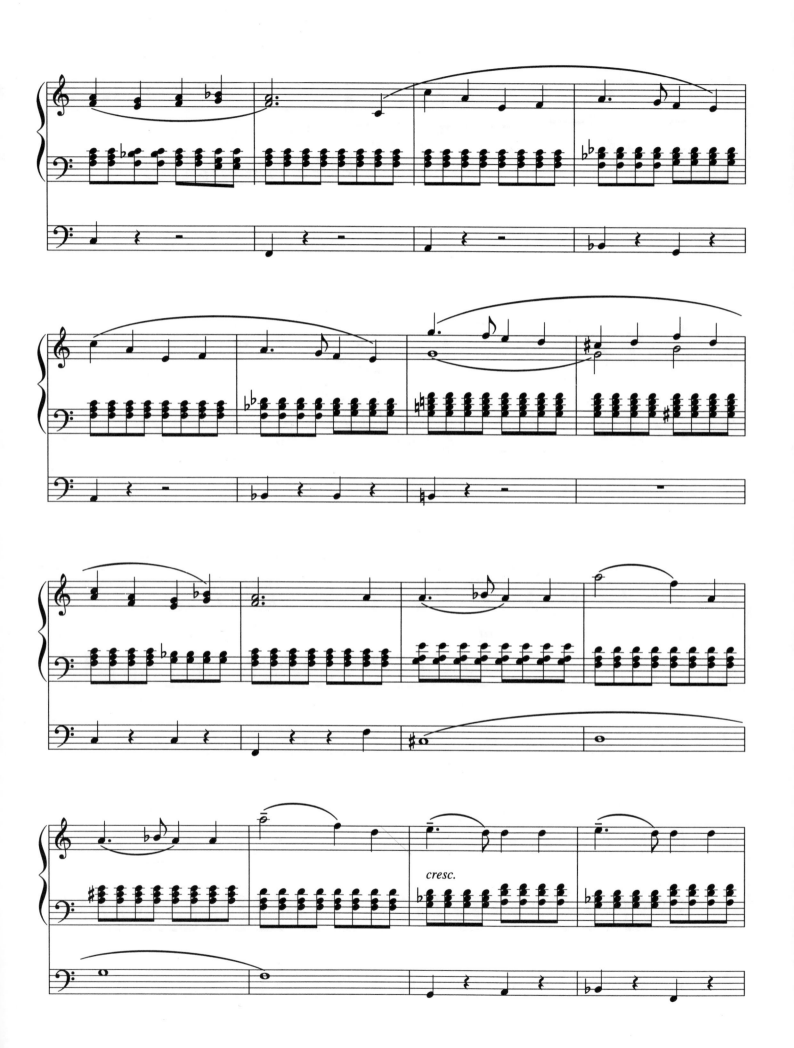

TWO TRUMPET TUNES AND AIR

Henry Purcell (1659-1695) arr. Noel Rawsthorne

Clarke

Allegretto (♩ = 86)

Flutes 8'2' *mp*

non legato

*

*

* If possible change registration for the repeats, with a similar dynamic.

Cebel

Allegro (♩ = 106)
Trumpets 8'4'

f non legato

Accomp.